I'VE BEEN MEANING TO TELL YOU

I'VE BEEN MEANING TO TELL YOU

ARIANA MOULTON

atmosphere press

Published by Atmosphere Press

Cover design by Felipe Betim
Cover art by Josh Moulton. www.joshmoultonfineart.com

Atmospherepress.com

This book is dedicated to survivors near and far.

"And the day came when the risk to remain tight in a bud was more painful than the risk it took to blossom."

— Anais Nin

*"No tears in the writer,
no tears in the reader."*
-Robert Frost

Contents

1

2

1

Broad Shoulders

If you're not from Chicago
you don't know the sinking city
a leaning lakefront angled in algae.

You don't know where Lakeshore Drive
hairpins at the Drake Hotel,
the chatty Uber driver told me.

You don't know the wild onion plant,
smells of its name "Chicagoua"
a whispering Potawatomi glanced

at the river whose bend never spoke
of the Sears Tower, cloud busting
in black steel, a pillar, two spires.

If you're not from Chicago you've
not needed an ankle length coat
for February strolls, that icy wind.

This Windy City speaks
of politicians, air filled,
those boasting times

when Ferris' Wheel wowed them,
steel spokes near Navy Pier,
a quartet in each car.

But you wouldn't have known of
our World's Fair unless Burnham
visited you in a dream,

whispering "Urbs in Horto"
a city in a garden of roots,
native and immigrant.

I never expected to
grow roots in Chicago,
This city of Broad Shoulders,
the city you don't know.

Finding Katie

I don't know where I slept last Friday,
or when my purse was emptied.
I'm Katie, I told them when they asked.
Four men in blue, one cradled me like a chair.

I'll never know that my hair splayed out
like snakes around my face, slithered and still.
My shallow breathing, my
velvet pants, too warm for June.

It was as if God himself lowered me
onto the summer pavement, no injuries,
no pool of blood. I traced myself in chalk
with one jagged pill.

Hovered over streets with
glittered synapses splashing into a
sunrise slumber. There I was.
Sleeping it off (I guess).

She didn't follow the ambulance
or ask me if I needed money.
But I know she must have been there,
like someone's mother.

She knew that I wanted to watch
the morning swallow the night,
look directly into the place
where no one goes.

Walk of Shame

Because the sprinkled sand reeks of beer and litter,
    eyes burn awake, a night of sweat, of smiles.

Chicago's lakefront cradles your colors.
    Those fake eyelashes flutter like night glitter
        because for you it's not Sunday morning.

Saturday night shoes, that fancier purse
    no match for the morning dew, the pecking geese.
        Your smoke-filled hair is happier than laughter's light.

You won't notice the cluster of Hispanic boys,
    their expensive bikes, trick turning
        camera catching this morning's high.

It's as if you've forgotten our city once reeked of onions
    our namesake too, Checagou.
        Gem by the lake.

If you could ride higher into yourself
    you'd see we're just a string of pearls
        along this saltless sea,

littered perfectly near a lake that's
    greatest at dawn.

Imperfectly Healed

What if someone told you
nothing was wrong with you?
You're perfect amongst the birds,
amidst January's
trees of lace.

Could you remember a time
without scratches?
Like tracks on a frozen pond,
a skater's trail.
Before you resonated resilience.

Rummaged forward, no flock
no protective "V" to fly in.
Feathers repair
themselves, the layers,
that gentle air.

No moral failings,
no flailing arms
a skater's outstretched leg,
in which hope is a muscle,
maneuvering frozen layers.

Built one cold front
at a time, no flawless
surface, your purpose
drawn.

Because no one seems
to say what you already know.
That everybody's beautifully
scratched.

Summer Doesn't Ask

When winter's not a threat
and humidity sticks, thick.
The cicada just knows
it's time to rumble buzz
this city by the thousands.
Don't ask me how the spider
knows its web dazzles,
the dew, geometry rising.
Don't ask me how many times
my body has bent, branch
swaying.
Summer bends like a question
no intention of ending, pretending
a morning's timeless.
Tomorrow the apple swells redder
in the hand of a child, excitement
tart on the tongue.
The youngest of them all.
We've collectively aged
mourning the dust
behind a mask
its tough to see me
stretch again.

Night Shift

She doesn't know she's waiting
to become her older sister.

But Friday plans commence,
leaving her alone in their shared room.

A deep breath as she eyes the vacant
desk chair, the lonely mascara.

She flops backwards
onto the white cotton duvet.

Letting herself sink into what
being 12 will feel like.

Because 9 doesn't seem
to shine like the gold strappy heels

waiting near the shelf.
She clips her hair back,

out of her face like her
sister does each morning.

Prays the mirror will show
an older face, one that's not

stuck in the fourth grade.
She applies that shade of pink,

the eyeliner too.

Because being young
feels like forever,

like waiting for Christmas
or your birthday,

when you'll finally open
a box that's yours.

He Blamed the Schools

He said the kid should have
been in school.
Where were his teachers,
his backpack
packed with books?
He said that cop will
never be the same,
the dust on his hands,
his family at home.
When bullets unpack
themselves in our alleys,
4 a.m. has no school bell,
no principal on watch.
He said the gang tattoo
was new, not healed
the 13-year-old arm,
a Latin King.
Wishes like black feathers
shatter streetlights
tonight, while downtown
braces for breakage.
Bridges erect above
Chicago's river, a divide
that once caught fire.
Flames licked
their way north,
then and now,
too many conflagrations.
Was it fear that fired

in that alley, or boys without
a playground,
no schedule to keep?

Check Mate

There's nothing more beautiful
than the brown woman in white.
Looking like a chess piece,
head to toe fabric,
hooded grace, facing east today.

The later sunrise stole the show
through cloud puffs of gray,
a cantaloupe glow.
I know what brings *me* to the water.

Her stillness, a gift to herself.
While our great lake swells,
flattens and punctuates
her stoic silhouette.
A marble woman.

It's as if singing called her closer,
told her to pray to the fading stars
ask them not to hide,
not to leave her in the light
for people to stop,

to wonder if God had
moved her there,
       check mate.

The Score

He didn't know what he was doing,
He couldn't see through liquid eyes.
His leather shoes on gravel slipped
His tongue, that grip was her demise.

He didn't know what he was doing,
Smoke surrounded him like twisted paint,
A shirtless sweat the creep, the crowd
A poor excuse for no restraint.

He didn't know what he was doing
when she stood in his dorm room door
the towel rack, his racing blood
that concrete floor.

He didn't know what he was doing
when she picked that apple sweet,
Her will, those fingers
knew this time it was hers to eat.

For blossoms decide to keep the score
and roots will not forget,
So deep the scratch,
the scar, the eye
appears
legit.

You Don't Have to Tell Me That

I think I need to tell
my eleven-year-old about
every pothole in the street.

Her shiny rose gold bike,
her latest chariot,
a sunrise ride with mom.

I think she wants me to
tell her when both ways are clear,
no waddling mallard to avoid.

Today the horizon's too gold.
She tells me it's beautiful,
through watering eyes.

I know I didn't need to tell her
where to look, the morning
does its job.

It's time. This time for her
to know that peace is
the glassy lake,

that paddler's stroke.
And knowing is enough.
One day she will breathe

her way through dewy grass
without me pointing left,
and cracks will
appear to her.

No One Hands Guns to Girls

It's not going to be her
  who pulls a trigger.

It's not going to be her
  who snaps.

She wasn't told to toughen up,
  grip harder onto the
    air between them.

It's not going to be her wrists
  cuffed in metal,
    bone aching phone call.

Her shackles hide,
  are inside.
    She traps herself.

Breaks her own stride.
  She won't be running
    from flashing blue.

The failure's obvious too.
  It's written in the dust,
    that scatters,
      that never settles.

She's not hiding
  a gun on her hip
    When her friends ask her
      to tread.

To meet up at a certain time,
    Millennium Park looks different
        when you can't find anyone you know

and bullets have left barrels hot
    Summer's about to unload.

If You Look Up

Because sometimes you look up
    and the sun has beaten you to the horizon,
        reminding you that all things end.

A season, a restless night.
    You'll never notice the tilt of the Earth,
        or time passing.

You won't feel it, like salt in your sneaker
    on this morning's frozen run.

Nor will it stop you from cursing
    wildly into the wind,
        those jealous branches.

When morning light spreads,
    a golden wash aims to quiet you.
        To soundproof your soul for a moment.

The watercolor air, the duckless harbor,
    and a friend or two's just right
        for telling you to look up.

Or to find your way forward through ice
    that's thick, no swaying masts,
        no rising sail to tell you nature's plan.

Our windy city still shadowed just right
    for eyes that choose to see.

To See It

She thought she didn't
deserve tiny beautiful things,
that lavender balloon with
the pink ribbon.

She wondered if digging her toes
in deep meant forgiving herself
for all the changing
of the tides.

She cannot find
beauty when she looks,
reflections never worked
in her favor.

We don't choose this life,
where sand blows sideways,
sings of footprints it has swept
away.

She knew no one could
protect her from her suffering.
Only *she* might call it that,
scream it into the wind.

And the balloon would
float away, so far.
So teeny, tiny she would have
to squint her eyes to see it.

The Pen, As Seen by Eight-Year-Olds

Inspired by "My Pen" by Christopher Myers

In Room 203 the girl with the short hair tells of
answers living inside her quill, of roots and vines

so green that forests of rain seep out.
Her socially distanced desk, her sanitized chair.

The boy in blue glasses writes of waves
that crash his childhood all over him.

An image that couldn't be thought of by a teacher,
who has already been pulled by the undertow.

The current, the climate keeping them six feet apart.
Far enough to invent a game of invisible thread,

or of paper boats that never reach land,
but flutter about on strings, small hands

the puppeteers, the architects who tell
everyone they love that they love them.

Or maybe they've just been muted too
long, behind a screen and a quiet pen

now begs them to be loud enough to
stop a virus, to splash ink on a page.

Do they know what history will say
about the etched butterfly, the bony hands?

And will a child remember that
feeling small is no more than a fear,
not forgetting that they can redraw

their faces today and forever.

Seeing the Circles

For Amy

Its thicker than her honey drips
round as concentric thoughts,
those rings inside her no one can count.

She wonders why the cardinal's lurking,
perching on the iron fence,
his feathered luck.

When pivoting never felt so tired he reappears,
awakens summer's song
for winter wanders distant.

Didn't the farmer's flowers appear
filtered through a lens today,
a dulled zinnia, brush strokes of dried wheat?

That beat below her, a dusty path
for her to draw her circle in,
shades of a kiss that's nameless.

She won't dismiss that scratch,
its crimson drop,
a mother's sap.

Believe Your Poets

I told my 12-year-old to lay down
   when she hears gunshots,
      to play dead in the dust of Oz Park.

Next to the patch of grass we
   play field hockey on, where we
      unleash our family dog.

I told another mother that it's not
   a matter of IF bullets will bleed into
      playgrounds or scatter the crowd at
         Lollapalooza…

She faced the sun the way she knows how,
   let it seep the sorrow,
      the pregnant air.

Her exhale told me not to ignore
   unsteady ground,
      the nauseous wind.

For it's when we see the underside of
   leaves that storms are near,
      and windows close themselves.

She didn't suggest we move out of Chicago,
   march on Washington,
      or find our country's quietest dirt road.

The air between us prayed,
and we believed
        it was listening.

When I Was Four

I used to ask if the dad would be home
when my mom took me to a friend's house.

I didn't want to see his scratchy face,
hear that louder voice.

But thirty years of forgetting
has made waves out of my body,

an ocean of thoughts spill
like milk, a cheerio mess.

I pay money to sift through
the emotional silt,

shaking around for a hint of gold,
invaluable stress.

Because remembering never seemed
so important, so urgent.

If it wasn't for the tides reminding me
that change bends with the earth,

I would put down that mirror,
    breathe into myself,
        release all questions,
            the non-memory of him.

"I hadn't so much forgot,
       as I couldn't bring myself to remember."

-Maya Angelou, **I Know Why the Caged Bird Sings**

There's something in the silence
taped across her face.
She blamed her voice,
her raven breath.
Bloodied hands and locked up rage,
the cage, the silenced iron.
The tattling air that locked him up,
the bruises weep the word, the must.
Causing her to tell.

To lock syllables away for five years straight,
below a throat shut tight,
where poems were brewing
In silent lines—
    Her future she would write.

Eventually she knew that it was the world
that made a mistake,
She could see through stinging eyes,
    Knowing, yes, knowing,
        Someday,
            she would rise.

Distress

If living in the city means that
you sleep on the pavement,
paper bag charity lined up,
doggy bags, your pillow of rags…

If living in the city means
a 3 a.m. hit and run,
metal bends, it swallows
no hovering witness…

If living in the city means
stolen packages, hopeful
sticky hands snatch Amazon
boxes beyond the tracks…

It wouldn't mean my bed's
comfort solves a thing,
no slumber of sorry,
no way I can fix this.

It wouldn't mean my airbag
could intercept a careening
evening in distress.

This blessed mess means blending
concrete lines, in time,
for the night to reverse,
no curse,

no way to rise.

Weighted Blanket

She knew her mind spoke
with a voice that wasn't hers,
telling her things she would
never think of, never imagine.

She knew not to listen,
when it was louder than light
between her ears,
ringing in silence.

It followed her like
a strand from a ball of yarn,
rolled alongside her
in the snow.

She looked for footprints
not her own to see if
anyone was carrying her,
moving her forward.

She only saw her own feet,
one in front of the other
reminding her she can't
run away from herself.

Reminding her that her mind
buries itself in the snow
from time to time,
leaving her counting snowflakes.

Glitter for Winter

I told you the harbor is empty
and forward feels like pushing
through a wall of snow.

Empty never looked
or felt like this—
like dark clear water

heavier than knowing
Winter's coming,
it's underneath.

The leaves are matted down
like rolled out dough disguised
in faded orange, forgotten yellow.

It won't rain light (or so you think)
for months and time will pass in
the deepest of ways.

Its absence we breathe
as December rolls in like a fog,
and we wish we could decorate the silence,

with glitter sounds of gold,
holding onto colors of yesterday,
blowing them off your hand

back into the water,
where as long as we stay awake
we'll see our eyes,
our unimaginable selves.

Make a Wish

How do you write a poem
about someone you didn't know?
Imagine into the untold corners.
Pretend you could see through
the stained-glass windows he left behind,
when the packages began to pile up
and the neighbors began to wonder.

How would you have known it was
the last time you would see him,
swaying down Fletcher Street,
a slow determined pace?

Maybe you would have made a wish
in that moment because the way seeing him
caught you off guard never quite made sense.

Like the time he told you he was from Turkey
and his twinkling eyes aged him backwards,
standing behind his chain link fence,
His crooked green and white house.

You never would have believed it if you heard
him whistling at midnight, a miniature watchman.
Who centuries ago would have been extinguishing
gas-lit streetlamps, clicking shoes on cobblestones.

Because for all you know he appeared out of all
of our imaginations, more mysterious than his unlit
living room, his murdered son.

And if you're lucky enough to have known him
and his love for the simplistic,
you too would close your
eyes longer than expected.

A Poem for Boystown

If you ever find yourself awake in Chicago's dream,
wander willingly through darkened side streets.

    Where Saturday seeps into Sunday, while silent disco lights rotate
    above Halsted Street.

The skinny one shouts, "I don't do that fake shit! I do it real."
4 a.m. cluster of mesh tights, high heels no regret.

    It's not a time to linger long, not much gets better as dawn
    knocks awake our nearby lake.

Glazed skin and muscles gleam as he gets into the stranger's car
with feet so bare, concrete careful.

    You wouldn't want to be seen unless you wore your leather too,
    or grew out your beard, left your shirt behind and marched to
        Roscoe &
Clark, smirking, peeling off from the group.

If you lift this city's blanket off when it's not looking,
you too will find the under-there, the night laugh sparkle.
    And maybe glitter will land,
        lifting you above Lakeview.

I Didn't Know How Much I'd Miss Her

She's daring me to *be* the harbor,
be waves of gray and
empty slips.

She's not coming back
to shore, to reassure me
of anything I thought I knew.

She's daring me to stand alone
to cherish my own harvest,
my own crisp joy.

I don't know when I'll stop
looking for her.
I pray I'll see her leaning mast.

When morning used to paint her
in shades of orange
she'd tell me where she'd been,

how it felt to have
    the anchor lifted,
        bow pointing east.

If She Waits

The girl in the third floor
window is mine.

Thick waves of long
honey hair.

Above Fletcher Street,
the peak of the house.

She's figured out she fits
in the window's shelf.

Learned her stillness
is a gift to herself.

She tells of a scampering
midnight rat, a glimpse.

If she waits long enough
a cat will appear.

Together they'll
whisper about the

girl behind the glass.
Can they rescue her?

Build her a ladder of
sticks for her to descend.

Her bare feet,
cold on wet cement.

Where would I have
wanted to go when I was 10?

Some place on a horse,
with a best friend, too.

Tonight I don't ask her
what brought her

to the window.
What's taken her gaze.

For it's her darkness
to fear, to imagine into.

When the rat becomes
a carriage horse.

Like in her books.
Where freedom means

never telling what you see,
what you hold onto.

Zen of Don't Know

My father is calling it a transition.
A process of change, from one
state to another.

Amongst the pines his
rhythmed gate proves
planning is for the birds.

We pass the rooster
whose morning call crows
out of synch this late afternoon.

In tune with nothing but itself.
The rooster calls us to pray with him,
to step carefully through grass

that's not been mowed
nor trimmed into
a circle of buddhas

who may call this time
Nirvana, the stilling of the fires,
red and rolling forward

like a season.

His seasoned spirit no match
for a word like "transition" that's
come to mean more than we know.

Out of Office

You can't hear it
when the moon's
limb passes through
the Earth's shadow.
It doesn't tell you
what it's going to do.
It doesn't warn you
that your eyes will
seem to play tricks,
and this lunar eclipse,
this blood moon
is a paper collage.
Nighttime scissors
snip a sliver of
wax paper,
big enough to
cover one eye,
big enough to
reveal change
you didn't know
was folded into a leaf
or a ballot, ink stained
with tomorrow's bodily
laws writing themselves
across the sky.
It's as if God himself
held the moon in His mouth,
tricking you into believing
you could repair all of this.
One piece of scotch tape at a time.

Reaching through the open window,
telling the stars to hide,
for they could be next in
line to vote the moon
out of office.

Sign Here

How many times has the email said
"Sign here to ban assault weapons?"
Near the red X like the scope used
to narrow in.

Have you huddled in a classroom corner
with 8 year old eyes asking you why?
Telling you they're afraid,
while your crouched legs shake.

Has your 13 year old learned of the carnage
before you did, telling you *Mom, there's*
been another school shooting,
while your eyes look beyond her unfocused.

Because it's all blurred like static,
and you can't remember names of towns
whose lawn signs tell of staying strong,
but disintegrate while bullets are bought.

No one asked you if you if there's room
in your teacher desk for a handgun,
next to the white out, the gold star stickers
you put next to each name.

And when the parents rifle through faces like paper,
searching for the one they know belongs to them,
the air screaming electric waves of doubt,
of deadly wonder.

Because You Asked

Henry in my class asks,
"What does silent sound like?"
Expecting me to have words,
syllables to slip over the air,
today in March when
the weather's confusing us.
I could tell him that silence
is an absence, like when no one
comes to your door.
Or maybe the quiet ache in
my leg from winter running,
isn't loud enough to stop me
in my tracks.
I want to explain to him
that he will listen with his
heart, it will feel things louder.
And when his cheeks flush
I know he's played beyond sound
like kids know how to do,
disrupting neighbors,
a stick rattling on an iron fence.
I want to ask him what's left in
his ears when his three siblings
aren't home, his nanny's away.
The hurried air, a novice story
he's writing. A boy that's a wizard
like him, riding on a broom through
bell towers, cheers from below,
a standing ovation.
I wish all could hear me when I

explain that someday those cheers
will be for him and that his question
speaks volumes.

Bill Maher Said

It's migrant season.
He lives in California
where the avocados
don't pick themselves,
dust covered, thick skinned.
His microphone doesn't have
a pit for him to fall into
in the night where he would
have to huddle with a brother,
a sweaty stranger
from further south.
The screen he's on saves
him from having to ride
in a truck's bed
laying down for days,
and Orion would be up above,
his belt, those stars pointing
towards the only option.
A politicized insecure
border that traces and erases.
Patrolled by recent graduates,
no other option.
No name other than "cages"
because anything that
locks keeps you in,
and out at the same time.
It would be a mistake
not to note that in Chicago
today a worker stepped aside,
made way for my

running dog and I,
as he waited for the
first bus of the morning.
The earliest Sunday shift.
Because work has no borders,
no lines in the dust when
family's left behind,
waiting for an envelope
of money. I smile of course,
unsure why there's
a pit in my stomach.

3

A Trusted Fall

Let me go,
Let me unclip
From this mind.

I've seen this reel,
The bell curve moods
That swing alone in time.

The fog the angst,
The feather dance,
Has crippled this desire,

For pavement knows,
And dust declares,
You can't burn women
Made of fire.

They brand themselves,
With skin scorched deep
And no one's there to save them.

A trusted fall,
With arms stretched wide,
And actions most condemn.

Its dormant light that drags and weighs
Heavy like a season,
The jail cell locked
The metal cold,
The mind commits its treason.

No Line Breaks

My father taught poetry
writing to prisoners
at the Great Meadow
Correctional facility.
Words belong to us all,
he didn't need to say.
I don't know how many
clearance forms he signed,
how many times they took
his fingerprints.
Those soft poet hands
don't remember.
I visited David,
my friend's brother.
Cook County Correctional
center, a federal prison.
Alliteration altered my vision,
Bulletproof panes of plexiglass.
He wanted to hear of the outside,
the over there.
What did Lake Michigan feel
like on bare feet?
How could he rewrite the
night he stood on the wrong
corner, with a friend
who didn't murder anyone?
No line breaks in his line up,
no metaphor for handcuffed
hands whose innocent
prints needed a pen, a piece of
paper to slip between bars.

Love Gets Folded

Nobody knows what you're looking for
at Belmont Harbor on Mother's Day.
The dog's already found mud to roll in,
a goose to piss off.

Nobody knew she wouldn't come back.
That sailboat named Nellie you may
have fallen for, oddly so. Her curves
that bow out strong.

It's the nearness of cardinals today,
that tell you what you need to know.
Flittering red in May's warmer rays.
Lucky when he lands near you.

He's saying that gone doesn't mean
what you think. It's just that love gets folded,
hidden into corners, anchored away.
Returning flocks can see the bigger picture.

Nobody said you were exempt from
Lake Michigan's deceptive glow,
a dust that floated by your door,
wasn't meant for you.

Wasn't meant to sail you through
hours of quarantined Netflix,
or under proverbial stones
to hide like the sugar ant
who crawls up your coffee
you can no longer taste.

And in the end, you'll find
that muddy sneakers track
their way back to a quiet street
where mothers are waking.

544 W. Fullerton Parkway

Just when you think you know
Chicago's grit–you see it
in January's darkest dawn.
It's there in siren blue,
an epileptic flash.
Before you heard them,
ear piercing careening corners.
You had just been wondering
how long it takes for Lake Michigan
to swallow a soul, to fold someone under.
First the barricade at Fullerton & Clark.
How casual the officer seemed.
Silhouettes westward down the block.
Residents in robes, a retriever on edge.
It's not often you see their hose
so massively clamped to the hydrant
nor should the neighborhood reek of smoke.
Four engines, two ambulances and that
extended ladder like a narrow bridge.
Flames don't decide which vintage
brownstone or antique attic to burn.
The smoke rolled upwards in gray,
crawled backwards in time to when our
alleys were wooden and horses pulled
engines, carrying that single dalmatian
used to keep the horses calm
when they were forced closer to flames.

Smoke Among the Willows

for Amy

How do you thank the woman
who speaks through the trees?
Bending as roots do,
below the dirt, the surface,
her hands in deep.

How would you wake her,
find her like smoke among
the willows? Dancing delicate
threads between oak and elm.

Trees don't ask for honey,
amber offerings, lengthening drips.
Blonde wisps of worry to break open
ancient wounds, the deeply scratched.

How could you know she'd lead
you through yesterdays?
Through the inside out.
To a place of connection
untangled.

When leaves speak for her,
she can let go, lay her body down.
Exhale those who came before.

I Must Go In

for Emily

What words to leave behind,
in fog that's rising?

What weakness clouds your death
be still, compromising.

Delicate air surrounds you white,
internal storm, capsizing.

A lantern tipped ignites the pen,
devising.

Words of wicked hope, that stack,
a breath revising.

A sister hovers, worry,
unsurprising.

For fortune found is fortune bound
a body arising.

Stones stacked in rows,
    epitaphs etched
        a woman surviving.

Through a Cloth Window

CNN isn't saying names
to protect the women.

My screen tells it in pictures,
a horror flooded runway.

Your country's gripping its children,
their terrified feet.

Burqas hang like lifeless bodies.
A mad rush the market's closing.

A grenade tossed outside of
Kandahar, a widow's dirt floor kitchen.

She wouldn't cook for the 15 men in beards,
their torturing stench.

I've never peered through windowed cloth,
hidden my daughters from a living hell.

If you're still enough like stone,
like you're already dead

would dark eyes find you,
jam their rifle into your jaw,

spit centuries of hate to dust,
duller than the knife he used

to quiet her?

It's her inner voice that's louder
than newsfeeds today.

For she is the storm,
a spirit can turn cloth into

a magic carpet, raise her up
above flooded runways.

Intention's Game

At least I have this:
Pen to paper.
Stone to foot.

At least I have this:
Cold hand angst.
Teary eyed soot.

At least I have these:
Frozen air dreams.
City street screams.

On top of which
it seems cheek to mouth
a manic scheme.

Oh night, oh ice
of inward extremes.
What lessons
relief could mean.

A hero, a bird
this inward spiral,
that look, that text
a cloud gone viral.

Wet cheeks cold with
last time's guilt.
A daughter now split,
no confidence rebuilt.

2 a.m. grows silent heavy,
My windless folly in
laughter's night,

Intentions
forgotten,
forgiven, despite.

The Witching Hour

The wakeful night of empty
concrete

Lake effect wind slaps
a city

Metal subway
screams descension

Frozen board
homeless

No dandelion dancers
No watchmen

The streetlight a torch
for a giant

The hour of nothing
The meanest quiet

No surprising death
No mild ending

hottest in fall

fall came in through the open window,
crisp apple sound.

Lake Michigan wants to
hold up a mirror to the leaves,

paint itself
in reds, reach back through time

to put out flames that licked our
polluted river

jumped from south to north
through people's dreams of

how broad our shoulders could get.

wagon filled, children pushing
papa in flames, sheet wrapping

cries.

mama says to meet her at the sands,
where heads appear like stones,

neck buried, eyelashes burned.

silver sand spoons digging,
doll smashed, marbles.

rolling rains came two days
later, smolder damp,
near Ashland.

Haiku

for Ferdia & Nora

Farmbar glows golden
resting upturned stools, knowing
Wellington will wake

Mercury's Morning

My father tells of life below zero,
of Sundays when he's up early too,
searching for a space heater whose hum

might be enough to warm the books
in his study until they open on their own
like paper leaves with words floating

up off the pages, whirling into that place
where his fingers write them back into
a line, a meandering metaphor

that might reach over his mountain gaps
to where his son is building a house of ice,
in the wake of Boston's snow bomb.

A rotunda of snow bricks, benches
built in for when frozen friends
will join them as the light slants in that way

that only it does in January's last days.
Will he write of Chicago's lake in frozen circles,
like craters rolling themselves in undulation?

Or will his frosted windowpane keep
him from listening to the landscape,
its frozen heartbeat, its narrowing gaze?

The Frame

It's no surprise the sun rose
in hues of pink today.
Cloud ribbons draped
parallel in vain.

You didn't come here
accidentally to see if you
could sneak inside the frame,
that glow upon your skin.

The horizon doesn't care
how long you gaze,
if you gasp at
morning's light.

Because it's April.
Winter winds lurk longer
than anyone
would like.

Have you ever tried to
rush a season?

Call it closer like a child.
Let whispers dance longer
than they should?

Tell Earth she's not on time,
late to her own show,
nature's curtain call.

Just Like That

And so it was that Nellie
    remained in the harbor.
The lake remembered to
    let her stay.
Forgetful winds passing
    her rolled up sails.

It's only the New Englander
    looking for words
crisp enough to paint her
    onto a page.
I wouldn't know what to say
    when sitting in her bow.

Her planks like a cradle,
    a rocking sway.
She doesn't worry about me
    noticing she's still there.
That yellow life ring bright
    with the anxiety of change.

I suppose leaves know where
    to go when our tideless lake
begins to still
    and mothers look for packed
away winter coats,
    a hand knitted cap.

I want to tell everyone I know
    to peer at Nellie one last time,

write her into their books,
    before winter hides
        her swaying masts.

Never Hurry

Sometimes all you see
in Chicago are bodies.
Not the V flocked geese in
sweet innocent flight.
But bodies in the sand,
chrysalis sheet wrapped tight.
Not the maple seeped in red
that glows in fall's late dawn.
But faded crimson shoes,
laces lifeless laying concrete flat.
No waves in shades of gray
will catch your eye along the shoreline.
Just doorway dormitories,
cardboard mattresses stacked
like bulldozed plans piled
haphazard landing.
No gentle breeze will distract
you into thinking of beauty pure.
For benches become bedrooms bare
the soot the smear the bodies tell
the story.

In the Time of the Guns

The police chief said
he couldn't say why the
car was pulled over,
blue lighted, city ignited,
female officer dead.

No background crime
this time, but you couldn't
get much higher than laughter's light,
this unplanned night.
He didn't say he brought a gun.

He didn't say he wanted to shoot
down the moon.

When 4 a.m. finds you still awake
nothing gets better,
going back would mean
a bullet in reverse,
let's rehearse.

An evening without guns in Chicago.
Give summer permission
to cradle us, no tighter grip,
no tension,
release that clip.

He didn't say he wanted to shoot
down the moon.

Don't take Lightfoot lightly
Monday morning officers mourning,
not a vigil, a stunned sea of navy,
when hugging is all
that keeps you
standing.

When She Stands Alone

for Amy

She had to be the tree.
    She had to seep between its grooves,
        a mother's sap,
                a fluttering leaf.

She had to speak for broken souls,
    quiet as the morning she found
        no shadow, no trunk
                for holding strong.

She knew her way to strength and patience
    would be through towers of oak,
        of elm, those box elders.

No air could tell her
    where the axe had come from,
        how loud the split had been,
                the crash of branches.

It's she who teaches leaves to forgive
    through watering eyes.

It's she who beats Earth's drum
    with feet that are bare.

The dirt,
    the dust,
        the ash at dawn.

Outside Your Door

for Bridget Blessing, in memory of Jonathan Blessing

Because it seems he stops for some,
and dirt to dust will fade to bone,
I find it necessary to remind you

That flowers grow down,
with roots deep somber.
A job suited for this Earth.

For tangled webs do rise with tides
and show themselves in shadows,
But glisten still will dew drops new

and jet planes overhead.

He knocks on doors in night's stillness,
seeking the seekers
whose promises kiss alone.

He can't burn those made of fire,
those with unquiet minds,
hearts of iron.

He won't see his own footsteps
because you carried him,
flesh cradle in all.

Acknowledgements

"Zen of Don't Know" originally appeared in *Poet's Choice*, "Paradise Poems," on January 5th, 2022.

"I Must Go In" originally appeared in *Wingless Dreamer* on March 22nd, 2022.

"Smoke Among the Willows" originally appeared in *Stoneboat Literary Journal* on April 19th, 2022.

When I was Four originally appeared in *Poetry South,* Issue 15, on August 8th, 2022.

No One Hands Guns to Girls originally appeared in *Wingless Dreamer,* "Midsummer's Eve," on August 11th, 2022.

"Time is the Thing That's Showing" originally appeared in *Wingless Dreamer,* "My Unheard September," September 12th, 2022.

"Out of Office" originally appeared in *Mantis,* "New Poetry," November 13th, 2022.

"Outside Your Door" originally appeared in *Assignment Literary Magazine,* April 16th, 2023.

About Atmosphere Press

Founded in 2015, Atmosphere Press was built on the principles of Honesty, Transparency, Professionalism, Kindness, and Making Your Book Awesome. As an ethical and author-friendly hybrid press, we stay true to that founding mission today.

If you're a reader, enter our giveaway for a free book here:

SCAN TO ENTER
BOOK GIVEAWAY

If you're a writer, submit your manuscript for consideration here:

SCAN TO SUBMIT
MANUSCRIPT

And always feel free to visit Atmosphere Press and our authors online at atmospherepress.com. See you there soon!

About the Author

Ariana Moulton is a 3rd-grade teacher and writer living in Chicago with her two daughters and husband. She grew up in Cornwall, Vermont, attended Bates College and has her master's from Columbia College. She is inspired by nature, politics, Chicago, and the people and landscapes of Vermont. Newer writing explores themes of aging, gun violence, and sense of place. Her writing appears in *Verity LA, Poet's Choice, Lucky Jefferson, Poem Village, What Rough Beast Covid 19 Edition* and others. Her first book, *Tracing the Curve* (Atmosphere Press) was published in 2021.